Bond

English

10 Minute Tests

9–10 years

Sarah Lindsay

OXFORD

UNIVERSITY PRESS

Test time: 0 ┈ 5 ┈ 10 minutes

Add the missing commas to these sentences.

1–2 On her way to school, Carys realised she had forgotten her glasses, ✓ 2
swimming things, reading book and recorder.

3–4 Dave and Tim struggled through the rain, slipping on rocks and ✓½ 1
stumbling through the mud, as they hurried to reach cover.

Complete the word sums. Watch out for the spelling changes!

5 depend + able _dependable_ ✓ **8** doubt + ful _doubtful_ ✓

6 early + er _earlier_ ✓ **9** likely + hood _likelihood_ ✓

7 cord + less _cordless_ ✓ **10** response + ible _responceible_ ✗
responsible

Give one word for each of these *definitions*. Each word begins with the letter p.

11 A code of letters and numbers at the end of an address to help with the sorting and delivering of mail.

pin ✗ Postcode

12 A coin.

pound ✓

13 A drawing or painting of someone, usually showing their head and shoulders.

picture ✗ Portrait

14 A male member of a royal family.

prince ✓

15 The sweet part of a meal.

pudding ✓

Write the following *adjectives* of comparison.

Example: quiet   *quieter*   *quietest*

16–17   heavy   _heavier_ ✓   _heaviest_ ✓

18–19   good   _gooder_ ✗ *better*   _goodest_ ✗ *best*

20–21   angry   _anger_ ✗   _angerest_ ✗ spelling

angrier   angriest

Complete each sentence using a different *adverb*.

22   They screamed _loudly_ . ✓

23   I swam _efficent_ . ✗ effortlessly / elegantly

24   We giggled _proudly_ ✗ helplessly / insanely

25   He whispered _quietly_ . ✓

Write the *plural* forms of these words.

26   roof   _roofs roofs_ ✓

27   circle   _circles_ ✓

28   lioness   _lioness_ ✗ lionesses

29   quantity   _quantityes_ ✗ quantities

30   shelf   _shelfs_ ✗ shelves

3

Total 17 / 30

Write the *contraction* for each of these.

1   have not   _haven't_ ✓

2   could have   _could've_ ✓

3   I will   _I'll_ ✓

4   will not   _willn't_ ✗   won't

Write each of these words correctly.

5   temprature   _tempeture_ ✗   temperature

6   mischivous   _misschevious_ ✗   mischievous

7   ocurred   _ocured_ ✗   occurred

8   apreciate   _apreciate_ ✗   appreciate

9   forign   _forighn_ ✗   foreign

10   existance   _existance_ ✗   existence

11   familar   _familiar_ ✓

12   cemetry   _semetry_ ✗   cemetery

13   aggresive   _agresive_ ✗   aggressive

14   garantee   _garenty_ ✗   guarantee

Add the missing double letters to each of these words.

15   a c c idental ✓   18   courge I t e ✗

16   begi n n ing ✓   19   a p p earance ✗

17   reco m m end ✓   20   tomo r r ow ✓

Add ary or ery to each of these to make a word.

21 nurs___ery___ ✓

22 annivers___ary___ ✓

23 scen___ary___ ✗ scenery

24 burgl___ery___ ✗ burglary

25 diction___ary___ ✓

26 deliv___ary___ ✗ delivery

27 imagin___ery___ ✗ imaginary

28 gloss___ery___ ✗ glossary

Each of these words has a missing silent letter. Rewrite each word correctly.

29 reath   ___reathe___ ✗ wreath

30 night   _____ ✗ knight

31 resin   ___resine___ ✗ resign

32 sene   _____ ✗ scene

33 autum   ___auture___ ✗ autumn

34 clim   ___clime___ ✗ climb

35 sord   _____ ✗ sword

Add a different hyphenated prefix to each of these to make a new word.

bi-	ex-	re-	by-	cross-

36 weekly   ___bi- weekly___ ✓ –

37 country   ___cross country___ ✓ –

38 colleague ___ex-colleague___ ✓ –

39 election   ___by-election___ ✓ –

40 enter   ___renter___ ✗ – re-enter

Read this extract carefully.

The Very Bloody History of Britain   *by John Farman*

1 **The Cunning Celts**

[The Celts] came here [Britain] in 650 BC from central Europe apparently looking for tin – please don't ask me
5 why! The Celts were tall, blond and blue-eyed and so got all the best girls right away. This, of course, annoyed the poor Britons even more, but there was not much they could do about it as they
10 only had sticks and fists to fight with. The Celts set up home in the south of England around Surrey and Kent – building flash wooden forts which the poor boneheaded locals could only mill
15 around in awe and envy.

Now England wasn't too bad a place to live for the next few hundred years (providing you were tall, blue-eyed and blond). Then in 55 BC the late Julius
20 Caesar – star of stage and screen – arrived with a couple of legions from Rome, Italy. The refined Romans were repelled, in more ways than one by the crude Celts, who by this time had turned
25 blue (from woad). They did, however, come back a year later with a much bigger, better-equipped army – and guess what – were repelled again.

55 BC – The Romans

30 You couldn't get away from the fact, however, that the Romans were much sharper than the Celts. They therefore decided that they'd infiltrate peacefully rather than invade; which was just a
35 sneaky Italian trick. How the Celts didn't notice the daftly-dressed Roman soldiers I'll never know.

AD 43 Boadicea

This gradual infiltration took longer
40 than expected and the Romans became rather impatient. Emperor Claudius sent another lot of legions to conquer us properly – which they did – properly! The only real trouble they encountered
45 was a strange woman warrior from somewhere near Norwich. Her name was Boadicea and, from the only available picture I've seen, she seemed to travel everywhere in a very snazzy horse-drawn
50 cart with blades sticking out of the wheels. This must have made parking in London rather tricky, which is probably why she burnt it to the ground. She went on to kill 70,000 Romans but, when
55 they started getting the better of things, poisoned herself.

**When In Britain Do As
The Romans Do**

If you can't beat a Roman, join him.
60 Gradually the hostile Brits came round to the Roman way of thinking. The smart ones even managed to make a few lire and live Hollywood-style, in centrally heated villas covered in naff mosaics.
65 The unsmart ones stayed in their hovels, being only serfs and slaves…. Soon everybody knew their place. Christianity was made the imperial religion and the first two centuries were to be among
70 the most prosperous and peaceful in England's history.

Answers these questions about the extract.

The Celts originally came from Central Europe

1   Where did the Celts originally come from?

They came from Italy.   *X*

2   How did the Britons react when the Celts arrived?

Britian was annoyed.   *The Britons were not happy ½ as the Celts were more skilled than them*

3   When did the Romans first arrive on British soil?

In 55 bc.   *The Romans first arrived on 55 BC. need sentence.*

4   Describe one way the Romans were different from the Celts.

The celts were weeker than the Roman Empier   *¼*

5   Who was Boadicea?

killed lots of Roman

A female soldier that travels a lot.   *½*

6   Why was Boadicea described in the extract as 'real trouble' (line 44)?

She was very strong and hard To convince.   *X*

7   What is meant by 'the hostile Brits came round to the Roman way of thinking' (lines 61–62)?

The strong soldiers were fighting back consilly   *X*

8   What is the meaning of 'prosperous' in line 72?

The most calm way.   *X*

9   Describe what it was like in Britain during the period of Roman rule.

You would get quiet poor and restricted.   *X*

10 Why do you think John Farman has titled his book 'The Very Bloody History of Britain'?

The celts and Romans were very serious and was very bloody and vilont.   *½*

Total 1¾/10

Test time: 0 | | | | | 5 | | | | 10 minutes

Add a *verb* to these sentences.

1 _grabbed_ my coat, it's raining.   Grab

2 _Thinking_, Tariq is in the next race.   Watch

3 _____, we have to get the car out the mud!   Push

4 _Running_ on the carpet, Kate.   Sit

5 _____ your breakfast quickly, or you will be late.   Eat.

Write the masculine gender of these words.

6   daughter   _female_   son

7   cow   _male_   bull

8   waitress   _female_   waiter

9   duck   _Male_   drake

10 Mrs   _female_   Mr

11 queen   _female_   king

Underline one *clause* in each of these sentences.

12 The children wanted to walk to school even though it was pouring with ✓
    rain.

13 Jess worked hard at her story and finished it just before playtime. ✓

14 Although the sun was hidden by the clouds the sunbathers still got ✓
    burnt.

15 Tom jumped with excitement when he was invited to David's party. ✓

16 The chicken clucked loudly after laying an egg. ✓

8

Write two *antonyms* for each of these words.

17–18 hot   _cold_ ✓   _freezing_ ✓

19–20 hard   _soft_ ✓   _smooth_ ✓

21–22 love   _hate_ ✓   _despise_ ✓

Write a word with the same letter string and the same pronunciation.

23 rough   _tough_ ✓

24 dough   _though_ ✓

25 thorough   _borough_ ✓

26 fought   _thought_ ✓

Complete these words using *tial* or *cial*.

27 confiden_tial_ ✓

28 artifi_cial_ ✓

29 finan_cial_ ✓

30 ini_tial_ ✓

Time for a break! Go to Puzzle Page 42 ▶   (9)   Total

Write these *abbreviations* in full.

1 TV   _television_ ✓

2 km   _kilometers_ ✓

3 UK   _United Kindom_   Kingdom

4 approx.   _approximately_

5 UFO   _~~unknown~~ flying ~~orte~~ Object_ *unidenhhgd*

Circle the words that can be used for either gender.

6–10

lioness   (teacher) ✓   (farmer) ✓

husband   (electrician) ✓   (nurse)

(lord) ✗   (mistress) ✗   uncle

(doctor) ✓   niece   (headmaster) ✓

Write two *synonyms* for each word.

			giggle
11–12	laugh	_chuckle_ ✓	_laughter_ ✓
13–14	shut	_close_ ✓	_locked_ block
15–16	frighten	_scared_ ✓	_terrified_ ✓
17–18	drink	_slurp_	_gulp_ ✓

Write the word for the young of each of these animals.

19 pig _piglet_ ✓

20 owl _owlet_ ✓

21 duck _duckling_ ✓

22 goose _gosling_

Write a *definition* for each of these words.

23 purchase _to buy something_

24 supervise _Help someone / to watch over_

25 rehearse _to practise something_

26 grumpy _angry bad dempered_

Mix and match these words to make four *compound words*.

foot   snow   ball   man

27 _snowman_ ✓

28 _football_ ✓

29 _snowball_ ✓

30 _footman_

11

Total

Write six words using a word and a suffix from each box.

observe	assist	confide

ant	ance	ent	ence

$\frac{5}{6}$

1–6   _observent_ _assistance_ _confidence_ _assistant_ _observant_ _confident_
    X

Put a tick next to the words spelt correctly and a cross next to those spelt incorrectly.

$\frac{2}{6}$

7   height   ✓

8   weild   X

9   relieve   ✓

10   deceive   X ✓

11   retreive   ✓ X   i before e except for c

12   cieling   ✓ X   retrieve
                        Ceiling

Write two sentences that use commas, brackets or dashes to indicate when something is in parenthesis.

13–14 _____

_____

15–16 _____

_____

Write two *onomatopoeic* words that describe the sounds that each of these make.

[handwritten: spelling wrn. whoosh ✓] *[handwritten: spelling ✗ splash]*

17–18   volcano   ___woosh___   ___splach ✓___

[handwritten: drip]

19–20   plug hole   ___swoo ✗___   ___guy ✗ gurgle___

Complete the table of *nouns*.

21–28

jealousy	herd	jacket	China
Meena	lifetime	gaggle	hate

Common nouns	Proper nouns	Collective nouns	Abstract nouns
Jacket ✓	China ✓	*herd* / meena ✗	gaggle ✗ jelousey
Jealousy ✗	Meena ✓	lifetime ✗	herd ✗ hate

[handwritten below: gaggle]

Add an *adjectival phrase* to complete each sentence.

[handwritten: brave and fearless]

29   The ___amazing ✗___ cockerel, protected his chickens from the fox.

[handwritten: warm and strong]

30   The washing dried quickly in the ___efficient hot sun and___

_____ wind.

Total **11** / 30

Test time: 0   5   10 minutes

Change the *verbs* in each sentence into more powerful verbs.

1   The dog **ate** its food hungrily.   *ravished / devoured*

2   The children **walked** to the park.   *ran / rushed*

3–4   Mum **said** it was time   *yelled*   *jump*
to **get** out of bed.   *stated*   *walk*

5–6   As the car **drove** past, it   *rushed*
frightened the lollipop lady.   *rode*   *terrified*

Write two *adjectives* to describe each of these *nouns*.

7–8   a _new_ , _cute_ baby   *beautiful*   *happy*

9–10   a _fresh_ , _clean_ car   *bright*   *shiny*

11–12   a _big_ , _thick_ fish   *slippery*   *silvery*

13–14   _clear_ , _blue_ sky   *blue*

Write two examples of each of the following.

15–16   *proper noun*   _Curran_   _Jake_

17–18   *preposition*   _Over_   _beside_

19–20   *adverb*   _coldly_   _amazingly_

21–22   *pronoun*   _He_   _she_

Use *adverbs* (for example perhaps, surely) or *modal verbs* (for example might, should) to write four sentences illustrating degrees of possibility. For example, *The shops might be open later.*

Underline the adverb or modal verb in each sentence.

spells

23–24 Pehaps, I might be able to go out with you.

25–26 Surely that can not be James is it?

27–28 Amazingly, the bus can stop at the next stop next to me. ✗

29–30 Can I come over perhaps after you did your work so with we can chill out?

Total

Read this extract carefully.

The Ghost of Tantony Pig   *by Julia Jarman*

1   *A house was being built in Hogsbottom Field, close to Laurie Gell's home.*

He strained to see in the darkness. There was definitely an animal in Hogsbottom
5   Field, peering into the trench. Its head was down and large ears covered most of its face, but clearly visible, glistening in the moonlight was the flat edge of a moist snout.

10   For a moment he wondered if he ought to do something about it, tell someone. But then he thought that a pig in a pigfield or an ex-pigfield wasn't exactly an earth shattering event, wasn't a reason to call
15   out the emergency services or even wake his mum and dad…But where had it come from, he wondered. Was it one of Arthur Ram's? Escaped from the new farm perhaps?

20   Now it was making its way along the bar of the H-shape, pausing every now and then to look into the trench and push with its snout.

'Yow!'

25   'No Gingie.'

The pig was deliberate and careful, skirting the other side of the H now, pausing from time to time to examine and push. Stop. Start. Stop. Start. Then left. Left again.
30   Then it was turning round, to come down the other side facing him. Its head swung up and it stood still for a moment, seemed to be looking at Laurie, straight at him, its eyes tawny-gold in the moonlight.

35   'YOW!'

'Gingie. Wait.'

It was walking again. *Walking*. His stomach lurched. He told himself not to be stupid. Of course it was walking. That was what
40   pigs did…And then it was running, not walking now, but rollicking towards the end of the field, where suddenly it vanished.

Vanished. That made it sound like a conjuring trick. Now you see it, now you
45   don't. Had he really seen a pig or was it a cement mixer which looked fat and round?

Who was he kidding? He caught sight of his white knuckles gripping the window sill. The silence was heavy. He felt as if he'd
50   been holding his breath for an impossibly long time. He opened his mouth and the air came out in a gush – and the wind began again, whipping up the soil.

Closing the window he made his way to
55   bed. Mrs Gingerbits pushed under the covers and settled herself in the curl of his stomach. She was comfortable, like a purring hot water-bottle, but he couldn't sleep. Just lay there listening to the wind.
60   Trembling.

…Shouts woke him. It was light. He'd slept late – and there was something wrong at the building site. A ready-mix truck had just drawn up. Laurie dressed and breakfasted
65   quickly, hurried over the road. The driver was still yelling at Charlie Hancock.

'You ordered a ton of concrete, mate, you're getting it!'

And Charlie, very agitated, was pointing at
70   the field. 'Where you gonna put it mate? Look at the so-called footings!'

Laurie was already looking. There was none. The site looked like a badly ploughed field…

Answers these questions about the extract.

1 How was Laurie able to see the pig in the darkness?

Laurie saw the pig as the moonlight shown on it. ✓

2 Why was Laurie surprised to see the pig where it was?

Laurie was surprised to see ✗ _a pig at night._ construction site

3 Why didn't Laurie wake his Mum and Dad to tell them?

Laurie didn't wake her parents ✗ _as she ✗ wasn't certain._

4 What colour were the pig's eyes? _Ginger_ ✗

5 Copy a sentence in the extract that lets the reader know how Laurie is feeling.

His stomach lurched. ✓

6 What is 'Gingie'? _The pigs name._ ✗

7 Why in line 49 is the silence described as 'heavy'?

It meant there is complete silence ✗ _and there is no movement._

8 Who is Charlie Hancock? _He is the owner._ ✗

9 What is the significance of the final sentence in the extract?

She had been a feild all day. ✗ _✗_

10 Describe how you think Laurie is now feeling at the end of the extract.

I think she is feeling calmer ✗ _as it had now ended._

TEST 9: **Mixed**

Underline the *connectives* in each sentence.

1 Thomas had a friend around for tea <u>but</u> Alex wasn't allowed one. ✓

2 Kay was late for the party <u>despite</u> leaving home on time. ✓

3 Bola lost his race <u>when</u> he tripped over his laces. ✓

4 The dog barked <u>and</u> made the horse rear up. ✓

④

Write a *definition* for each of these words.

5 opinion — *Your thing you think is right*

6 confide —

7 truce — *Stop fighting* ✓

8 incident — *something bad happened.*

9 sudden — *out of nowhere.* ✓

③

Rewrite these sentences without the *double negatives*.

10 There wasn't no footballs to play with.

There wasn't footballs to play with. ✗

11 They didn't wear no school uniform on the trip.

They didn't wear school uniform on the school trip. ✓

12 There wasn't no recorder lesson today.

There wasn't a recorder lesson today. ✓

13 The train didn't arrive early at no platform.

The train didn't arrive early at the platform. ✓

③

18

Underline the correct *verb* form in each sentence.

14 The book (<u>fell</u>/fall) open at the page listing magic spells. ✓

15 When it snowed Raj (sweeps/<u>swept</u>) the drive. ✓

16–17 The groom (<u>was</u>/were) (<u>drove</u>/driven) to the church. ✓ ✓

18 Hannah (<u>found</u>/find) her homework just in time to hand it in. ✓

 ⑤

Circle the words which have a soft g.

19–24

geese   magic   legend

(register) ✓   (wrong) ✗

(playground) ✗   enlarge   dragon

dungeon   (disregard) ✗

mirage ✓   (ghost) ✗

①

Write whether these sentences are written in the past, present or future *tense*.

25 I am stroking my cat.   *present* ✓

26 I will eat my tea.   *future* ✓

27 I played football.   *past* ✓

28 I made pancakes.   *past* ✓

29 I might tidy my room.   *future* ✓

30 I am exhausted.   *present* ✓

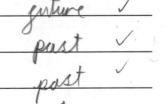 ⑥

Total 22/30

TEST 10: **Sentences**

Rewrite these sentences, adding the missing punctuation and capital letters.

1–6 did you get my e-mail gareth asked

"Did you get my e-mail?" Gareth asked. ✓

7–10 nina now she was feeling better had arranged to meet her friends

Nina (now she was feeling better) ✗ ②
had arranged to me her friends.

11–16 would you like some sweets asked deano

"Would you like some sweets?" asked Deano. ✓

Add 'did' or 'done' to each sentence to make it correct.

17 Ivan ___did___ his homework as soon as he was given it.

18 "I'm sure we have ___done___ the right thing," confirmed Helen. ✓

19 "___Did___ you know we had to bring a packed lunch today?" asked Tim. ④

20 They were sure they had ___done___ enough to win the competition. ✓

Write these sentences as *reported speech*.

21 "I'm glad you are coming with us, Aunty Sue," said Alex.

Alex said that she was glad
Auntie Sue came. ✓ ②

22 "We must remember our coats," Mum reminded the children.

Mum remined the children ✓
to take there coats.

Write four sentences, each with a relative clause beginning with the following words.

23 who

Jack, who was five, puked on the soga. ✓

(annotation above: fell in the garden .)
(annotation below: X)

24 which

Jake (which was Irish) loved
to sing and dance.

25 that

Jude - that was friends with everyone -
bought cake for the party.

(annotation: Comma? X)

26 where

James (where was in spain)
sun bored outside - before being X
trenched on.

(annotation: ①)

21

Total 9/26

Underline the correct *homophone* in each bracket.

1–2 The (bough/bow) of the boat collided with the (bow/bough) of the tree. ✗

3–4 Aimee's cut on her (heal/heel) didn't take long to (heal/heel). ✓

5–6 The (cellar/seller) sold his goods from the (cellar/seller). ✓

Underline the *pronouns* in the following passage.

7–11 ✓

They rushed over the rocks, desperate to get to safety before the
waves came in and cut them off from the path ahead. Henry cried as
he slipped and hurt his arm. It was wrapped in a jumper, as there was
no time for anything else.

Underline one word in each group which is not a *synonym* for the rest.

12	right	decent	honest	untrue	fair ✓
13	quiet	direct	peaceful	calm	tranquil ✓
14	guard	protect	defend	shield	pursue ✓
15	convey	clever	intelligent	smart	brainy ✓
16	offend	question	quiz	ask	interrogate ✓

Rewrite these sentences changing them from *plural* to *singular*.

17–18 The puppies raced towards the balls.

The puppy raced towards the ball. ✓ ②

19–23 They ate the ice-creams quickly as they dripped down their arms.

They ate the ice-cream quickly as they dripped down their arm. ✗

Add a *suffix* to each of these to make new words.

24 end ___less___ ✓

25 help ___ful___ ✓ ③

26 colour ___ful___ ✓

Add *tious* or *cious* to complete the words.

27 scrump___tious___ ✓

28 mali___cious___ ✓ ③

29 flirta___tious___ ✓

30 fero___tious___ ✗ ferocious

Total 22/30 2̶7̶

Test time: 0 | | | | | 5 | | | | | 10 minutes

Write the *root word* of each of these words.

1 redevelop _____ *develop* ✓

2 unanswerable _____ *answerable* ✗

3 prejudge _____ *judge* ✓

4 amusement _____ *amuse* ✓

5 untidy _____ *tidy* ✓

6 peaceful _____ *peace* ✓

7 electrician _____ *electric* ✓

8 interconnect _____ *connect.* ✓

(7)

Add able or ible to each of these to make a word.

9 excit__*able*__ ✓   13 flex__*ible*__ ✓

10 poss__*able*__ ✗ *possible* 14 divis__*able*__ ✗ *divisible*

11 inflat__*ible*__ ✗ *inflatable* 15 reli__*able*__ ✓

12 resist__*able*__ ✗ *resistible* 16 excus__*ible*__ ✗

(3)

Each of these words has an unstressed vowel missing. Rewrite each word.

17 histry _____ *history* ✓

18 avalable _____ *available* ✓

19 lesure _____ *leasure* ✗ *leisure*

20 vegtable _____ *vegatable* ✗ *vegetable*

21 jewellry _____ *jewellery* ✓

22 diffrent _____ *different.* ✓

(4)

24

Answers

Answers will vary for questions that require children to answer in their own words. Possible answers to most of these questions are given in *italics*.

Test 1: **Mixed**

1–2 On her way to school Carys realised she had forgotten her glasses, swimming things, reading book and recorder.

3–4 Dave and Tim struggled through the rain, slipping on rocks and stumbling through the mud, as they hurried to reach cover.

5	dependable	**8**	doubtful
6	earlier	**9**	likelihood
7	cordless	**10**	responsible

11 postcode
12 pound, penny
13 portrait
14 prince
15 pudding
16–17 heavier, heaviest
18–19 better, best
20–21 angrier, angriest

22	*loudly*	**27**	circles
23	*gracefully*	**28**	lionesses
24	*helplessly*	**29**	quantities
25	*quietly*	**30**	shelves
26	roofs		

Test 2: **Spelling**

1	haven't	**17**	recommend
2	could've	**18**	courgette
3	I'll	**19**	appearance
4	won't	**20**	tomorrow
5	temperature	**21**	nursery
6	mischievous	**22**	anniversary
7	occurred	**23**	scenery
8	appreciate	**24**	burglary
9	foreign	**25**	dictionary
10	existence	**26**	delivery
11	familiar	**27**	imaginary
12	cemetery	**28**	glossary
13	aggressive	**29**	wreath
14	guarantee	**30**	knight
15	accidental	**31**	resign
16	beginning	**32**	scene

33	autumn	**37**	cross-country
34	climb	**38**	ex-colleague
35	sword	**39**	by-election
36	bi-weekly	**40**	re-enter

Test 3: **Comprehension**

1 The Celts came from central Europe.

2 *The Britons weren't happy about the arrival of the Celts, though were in awe of their superior skills.*

3 The Romans first arrived in 55 BC.

4 *The Romans were more intelligent / more organised / better equipped than the Celts.*

5 *Boadicea was a female Celt who was a threat to the Romans.*

6 *Boadicea is described as 'real trouble' as she managed to lead a force against the Romans that killed many of the Roman soldiers.*

7 *The unhappy Britains that were invaded by the Romans eventually decided it was better to work with the Romans than against them.*

8 *successful, especially with money*

9 *It was a peaceful period in history when general living conditions improved for many.*

10 *John Farman titled his book as he did, as there appear to have been many 'bloody' battles to win control of Britain through different periods in history.*

Test 4: **Mixed**

1	*Grab*	**7**	bull
2	*Watch*	**8**	waiter
3	*Push*	**9**	drake
4	*Sit*	**10**	Mr
5	*Eat*	**11**	king
6	son		

12 The children wanted to walk to school OR even though it was pouring with rain.

13 Jess worked hard at her story OR and finished it just before playtime.

14 Although the sun was hidden by the clouds OR the sunbathers still got burnt.

15 Tom jumped with excitement OR when he was invited to David's party.

16 The chicken clucked loudly OR after laying an egg.

17–18 *cold, freezing*
19–20 *soft, easy*
21–22 *hate, dislike*

23	*tough*	**27**	confidential
24	*though*	**28**	artificial
25	*borough*	**29**	financial
26	*thought*	**30**	initial

Test 5: **Vocabulary**

1 television
2 kilometre
3 United Kingdom
4 approximately/approximate
5 unidentified flying object
6–10 teacher, farmer, electrician, nurse, doctor
11–12 *giggle, chuckle*
13–14 *block, close*
15–16 *scare, terrify*
17–18 *guzzle, gulp*

19	piglet	**21**	duckling
20	owlet	**22**	gosling

23 *to buy something*
24 *to watch over (a task, activity or person) to make sure everything runs well*
25 *to practise something*
26 *bad-tempered*
27–30 football, snowball, snowman, footman

Test 6: **Mixed**

1–6 observant, observance, assistant, assistance, confident, confidence

7	✔	**9**	✔	**11**	✗
8	✗	**10**	✔	**12**	✗

13–16 Two sentences that use either commas, brackets or dashes to indicate something is in parenthesis.

17–18 *whoosh, crackle*

19–20 *glug, drip*

21–28

Common nouns	Proper nouns
jacket	China
lifetime	Meena
Collective nouns	**Abstract nouns**
herd	jealousy
gaggle	hate

29 *brave, fearless and determined*

30 *strong and warm*

Test 7: **Grammar**

1 *gulped, gobbled*

2 *rushed*

3–4 *yelled; struggle, jump*

5–6 *raced; terrified*

7–8 *beautiful, happy*

9–10 *bright, shiny*

11–12 *slippery, silvery*

13–14 *blue, cloudy*

15–16 *Wales, Queen Elizabeth*

17–18 *in, after*

19–20 *softly, suddenly*

21–22 *she, they*

23–30 Four sentences, each using an adverb or modal verb to illustrate degrees of possibility, e.g. The shops *should* be open tonight.

Test 8: **Comprehension**

1 *Laurie was able to see the pig because it glistened in the moonlight.*

2 *He was surprised to see the pig because the pig was wandering around a building site.*

3 *Although Laurie realised he was watching something out of the ordinary, he also realised that it wasn't so important that he needed to wake his parents.*

4 *tawny-gold*

5 *'His stomach lurched'; 'He caught sight of his white knuckles gripping the window-sill'.*

6 *Laurie's cat Mrs Gingerbits.*

7 *The silence is described as 'heavy' because it is an uncomfortable silence, loaded with worry and concern for Laurie.*

8 *the builder*

9 *It proved that Laurie had seen a pig because the land was destroyed by the pig's rooting around.*

10 *Your child's description of how Laurie might now be feeling, e.g. frightened, worried, shocked.*

Test 9: **Mixed**

1 Thomas had a friend around for tea <u>but</u> Alex wasn't allowed one.

2 Kay was late for the party <u>despite</u> leaving home on time.

3 Bola lost his race <u>when</u> he tripped over his laces.

4 The dog barked <u>and</u> made the horse rear up.

5 *a statement of ideas or beliefs*

6 *to trust someone with a secret*

7 *an agreement between two parties to stop fighting for a certain length of time*

8 *an event or happening*

9 *happening quickly or unexpectedly*

10 There were no footballs to play with / There weren't any footballs to play with.

11 They didn't wear school uniform on the trip.

12 There wasn't a recorder lesson today. / There was no recorder lesson today.

13 The train didn't arrive early at the platform.

14 fell   **15** swept

16–17 was; driven

18 found

19–24 magic, legend, register, enlarge, dungeon, mirage

25 present   **28** past

26 future   **29** future

27 past   **30** present

Test 10: **Sentences**

1–6 "Did you get my e-mail?" Gareth asked.

7–10 Nina, now she was feeling better, had arranged to meet her friends.

11–16 "Would you like some sweets?" asked Deano.

17 did   **19** Did

18 done   **20** done

21 *Alex said he was glad Aunty Sue was coming with them.*

22 *Mum reminded the children not to forget/to remember their coats.*

23–26 Four sentences that include a relative clause using the listed words, e.g. That's the girl who lives near my uncle.

Test 11: **Mixed**

1–2 bow bough

3–4 heel heal

5–6 seller cellar

7–11 <u>They</u> rushed over the rocks, desperate to get to safety before the waves came in and cut <u>them</u> off from the path ahead. Henry cried as <u>he</u> slipped and hurt his arm. <u>It</u> was wrapped in a jumper, as there was no time for <u>anything</u> else.

12 untrue   **15** convey

13 direct   **16** offend

14 pursue

17–18 The puppy raced towards the ball.

19–23 S/he ate the ice-cream quickly as it dripped down his/her arm.

24 *endless, ending*

25 *helpful, helper, helping*

26 *colourless, colourful*

27 scrumptious   **29** flirtatious
28 malicious   **30** ferocious

TEST 12: Spelling

1 develop   **21** jewellery
2 answer   **22** different
3 judge   **23** They're
4 amuse   **24** there
5 tidy   **25** their
6 peace   **26** There
7 electric   **27–28** They're
8 connect   their
9 excitable   **29** veil
10 possible   **30** height
11 inflatable   **31** foreign
12 resistible   **32** cashier
13 flexible   **33** relief
14 divisible   **34** receipt
15 reliable   **35** flatter
16 excusable   **36** preferring
17 history   **37** busier
18 available   **38** transferred
19 leisure   **39** referred
20 vegetable   **40** relieved

TEST 13:

1 We don't know. It was written anonymously.
2 They sang.
3 *She wanted to wear something more practical outside.*
4 white
5 caught sight of
6 *She wanted a freer, or more exciting life.*
7 *The lord felt upset and surprised. He wanted to try to persuade her to come back home.*
8 *messy, dirty, unclean, untidy*
9 *the language it is written in, the description of the servants, horse, home etc.*
10 *happy, relieved and free to have left the home where she obviously felt unhappy*

TEST 14: Mixed

1 pizza – Italy
2 boomerang – Australia
3 restaurant – France
4 pyjamas – India
5 adverb
6 verb
7 preposition
8 abstract noun/noun/verb
9 pronoun
10 adjective/verb
11 *Chloe asked if they could go swimming.*
12 *The Bayliss family complained that they always have fish fingers for tea.*
13 *Dad suggested they drive past Buckingham Palace.*
14 *Elizabeth laughed, saying she loved pony riding.*
15 misquote   **18** dislodge
16 mishandle   **19** misspell
17 dismount
20–30 "I feel so tired," complained Jim.
"That's because it is one o'clock in the morning!" said the babysitter.

TEST 15: Vocabulary

1 impossiblility   **6** smart
2 irritable   **7** smirk
3 island   **8** smoke
4 ivy   **9** smother
5 investigate   **10** smuggle
11–14 *computer, compact disc, ipod, mobile phone, television*
15 *heehaw*   **17** *honk*
16 *roar*   **18** *cluck*
19–20 *untidy, messy*
21–22 *sad, unhappy*
23–24 *weak, feeble*
25–26 *damp, wet*
27 cloud   **29** fence
28 cats   **30** music

TEST 16: Mixed

1 HRH   **3** Dec
2 DIY   **4** PM

5 OAP   **9–10** to, to
6 PO   **11** two
7 too   **12** to
8 Too
13–16 "Time for your piano lesson," Mum called. (or!)
17–20 "Where have you put my phone?" asked Rebecca.
21 *sparkly, glamourous*
22 *terrified, prickly*
23 *mad, strict*
24 *empty, bustling*
25 *The rain poured but they still had a BBQ.*
26 *There was a fire in the school hall although it didn't do much damage.*
27 *Jake threw the ball and it landed in someone's garden.*
28 disrespect   **30** whisper
29 daft

TEST 17: Grammar

1–8

Common nouns	Proper nouns
insects pets	Jake Tyrone
Collective nouns	**Abstract nouns**
swarms colonies	dislike fear

9 *the old and musty book*
10 *the long, hot and busy summer*
11 *the fearless and amazing acrobat*
12 *the beautiful and interesting country of India*
13 *a lovely, old family photograph*
14 *because*
15 *although*
16 *but*
17 *as*
18 *so*
19–20 Everyone watched anxiously as the rope was lowered over the edge of the cliff.
21–22 The children wandered off gloomily despite being given some money to spend.

23–24 Nazar worked (happily) knowing as soon as he'd finished cleaning the car he could go <u>inside</u> to watch the rugby match.

25–30 *Three sentences, each sentence containing two possessive pronouns, e.g. <u>Ours</u> is bigger than <u>theirs</u>.*

TEST 18: Comprehension

1 Nairobi
2 (1) *dirt instead of paved roads* (2) *background noise of cockerels and cows instead of car horns and radios*
3 *the daughter of Boniface and Pauline Kamaus*
4 *one's native language/ the language a person first learns to speak*
5 *Many of the plants grown in Murang'a differ to those grown here because of the different climate.*
6 *Pauline felt comfortable back home with her parents and possibly liked getting away from the busy city.*
7–8 *Joyce and Sharon's grandparents must get their water from a stream and grow their own food. Most grandparents in England get their water from taps in their house and buy food in shops.*
9 *If they moved back to the country, getting a job to earn enough money to take care of the young family would be much harder than it is in the city.*
10 *the watching of TV, enjoying time with cousins, staying with grandparents etc.*

TEST 19: Mixed

1	*section*	6	torches
2	*unoccupied, empty*	7	princesses
3	*selfish*	8	thieves
4	*obvious*	9	bikes
5	*recall*	10	valleys

11	suffixes	21	You'll
12	under	22	mustn't
13	at	23	Let's
14	with	24	could've
15	above	25	I'd
16	on	26	*though*
17	dramatise	27	*weight*
18	solidify	28	*grown*
19	thicken	29	*hour*
20	fertilise	30	*door*

TEST 20: Sentences

1–4 *Two sentences, each with two correctly marked commas, e.g. Katy put her pencil, pen, ruler and sharpener in her backpack.*
5 *It is time to meet in the park.*
6 *We are going on holiday to Devon.*
7 *Liverpool won the Premiership.*
8 *The school is closed because of the snow that fell last night.*
9 *The cows are milked twice a day.*

10	are	12	is	14	Is
11	are	13	is	15	are

16–28 "What time does the film start?" asked Brenna.
She was worried they wouldn't have time to buy popcorn before it started.
"We have plenty of time," her dad reassured her.

Puzzle ❶

sausage – usage, age, sage, us, sag, a
wardrobe – ward, robe, rob, war, be, a
mathematics – math, at, the, he, them, mat, hem, tic, tics, thematic, thematics, a
scarecrow – scar, scare, car, row, are, crow, care, a
coincidentally – coincide, coincidental, dent, dental, tall, den, ally, all, incident, incidental, incidentally, tally, in, coin, a

Puzzle ❷

An adjective beginning with each letter of the alphabet – 'x' will be the biggest challenge and a dictionary could be used to help with this one!

Puzzle ❸

Your child's own answers to a number of word problems e.g.
   marmalade *maroon marry mask mass master match material maths matter mattress maximum mayor meadow mean measles* **measure**
A word with all vowels = *aeronautics*

Puzzle ❹

north = thorn
parties = pirates
vowels = wolves
team = meat, mate, tame
eighth = height
thicken = kitchen
Three anagrams chosen by your child

Puzzle ❺

silly – sensible
official – unofficial
dissatisfied – happy
huge – tiny
incorrect – right
unclear – legible
smooth – rough

Write there, their or they're in each gap.

23 ___Their___ going to be late. ✗

24 We must be nearly ___there___ by now! ✓

25 We'll collect ___there___ sleeping bags on the way home. ✗

③

26 ___Their___ seems to be a problem with that car. ✗

27-28 ___They're___ great friends but they argue about ___their___ favourite football teams all the time! ✓

Add ie or ei to each of these to make a word.

29 v_i_e_l ✗

30 h_e_i_ght ✓

31 for_i_e_gn ✗

①

32 cash_e_i_r ✗

33 rel_e_i_f ✗

34 rec_i_e_pt ✗

Complete these word sums. Watch out for the spelling changes!

35 flat + er = ___flatter___ ✓

36 prefer + ing = ___preferring___ ✓

37 busy + er = ___busier___ ✗   busier

38 transfer + ed = ___transfered___ ✗   transferred   ②

39 refer + ed = ___refered___ ✗   referred

40 relief + ed = ___reliefed___ ✗   relieved

Read this poem carefully.

The Wraggle Taggle Gypsies

1 There were three gypsies a-come to my
door,
And down-stairs ran this lady, O!
One sang high, and another sang low,
5 And the other sang, Bonny, bonny,
Biscay, O!

Then she pulled off her silk finished
gown
And put on hose of leather, O!
10 The ragged, ragged rags about our door –
She's gone with the wraggle taggle
gypsies, O!

It was late last night, when my lord
came home,
15 Enquiring for his a-lady, O!
The servants said on every hand:
'She's gone with the wraggle taggle
gypsies, O!'

'O saddle to me my milk-white steed,
20 Go and fetch me my pony, O!
That I may ride and seek my bride,
Who is gone with the wraggle taggle
gypsies, O!'

O he rode high and he rode low,
25 He rode through woods and copses too,
Until he came to an open field,
And there he espied his a-lady, O!

'What makes you leave your house and
land?
30 What makes you leave your money, O!
What makes you leave your new-wedded
lord;
To go with the wraggle taggle gypsies,
O!'

35 'What care I for my house and my land?
What care I for my money, O?
What care I for my new-wedded lord?
I'm off with the wraggle taggle gypsies,
O!'

40 'Last night you slept on a goose-feather
bed,
With the sheet turned down so bravely,
O!
And to-night you'll sleep in a cold open
45 field,
Along with the wraggle taggle gypsies,
O!'

'What care I for a goose-feather bed,
With the sheet turned down so bravely,
50 O!
For to-night I shall sleep in a cold open
field,
Along with the wraggle taggle gypsies,
O!'

Anon.

26

Answer these questions about the poem.

1 Who wrote this poem? _Bonny wrote the poem._ ✗

2 What did the gypsies do at the lady's door?

The gypsies sang at the door. ✓

3 Why do you think the lady took off her silk gown?

The lady took of the silk gown to put on the hose of leather. ✗

4 What colour was the lord's horse?

The lords horse was white. ✓

5 What does the word 'espied' (line 27) mean?

It means that she now wants to do something someone said. ✓

6 Why did the lady leave with the gypsies?

The lady left with the gypsies as she didn't get to the wedded lord. ✗

7 Describe how the lord felt about his wife leaving.

The lord felt when his wife left was upset and alone. ½

8 What impression does the phrase 'wraggle, taggle' give you about the gypsies?

The phrase gives me an impression of a wacky vibe. ✗

9 How do we know this poem was not written in the present day?

I know it is made in an older time as it says O!. ✗

10 At the end of the poem, how do you think the lady is feeling? Why?

She feels relaxed and peaceful. ✓

Total $3\frac{1}{2}$ /10

TEST 14: **Mixed**

Test time: 0 .... 5 .... 10 minutes

Draw lines to link each word with the country from which it is borrowed.

1 pizza   Australia ✓

2 boomerang   India ✓

3 restaurant   Italy ✓

4 pyjamas   France ✓

④

Which part of speech is each of these words?

5 beautifully   _adverb_ ✓

6 wrote   _verb_ ✓

7 behind   _preposition_ ✓

8 love   _abstract noun._ ✓

9 they   _pronouns_ ✓

10 blunt   _adjective_ ✓

⑥

Change these sentences into *reported speech*.

11 "Can we go swimming?" Chloe asked.

Chloe asked if she can go swim. ✓ ½

12 "We always have fish fingers for tea," complained the Bayliss family.

The _Bayliss family complained that they always have_ ½ _fish fingers._ ✗

13 "Let's drive past Buckingham Palace," suggested Dad.

Dad suggest to drive past Buckingham Palace. ✓

14 "I love pony riding!" laughed Elizabeth.

Elizabeth laughed as she said she loves pony ✓ _riding._ ✗

28

②

Select the *prefix* mis or dis for each of these words.

15 ___mis___ quote ✓

16 ___mis___ handle ✓

17 ___dis___ mount ✓

18 ___dis___ lodge ✓

19 ___mis___ spell ✓

⑤

Rewrite the following correctly.

20–30 i feel so tired complained jim that's because it is one o'clock in the morning said the babysitter

"I feel so tired" complained Jim.
"That's because it is one o'clock
in the morning!" said the babysitter. ✓

⑩

27½/36

Total

Write one word for each *definition*. Each word begins with the letter i.

1   Something that cannot be done under any circumstances. _*imposible*_

2   Grumpy and easily annoyed. _*irritating*_

3   A piece of land surrounded by water. _*island*_

4   A leafy, evergreen plant that can climb up walls. _*ive*_

5   To look into something or someone. _*investigating*_

Write these words in *alphabetical order*.

smirk   smother   smart   smuggle   smoke

6   _*smart*_

7   _*smirk*_

8   _*smoke*_

9   _*smother*_

10   _*smuggle*_

Write four words that have been invented in the last 100 years.

11   _*computor*_

12   _*ipad*_

13   _*air pods*_

14   _*nintendo switch.*_

Write an *onomatopoeic* word for the sound that each of these animals makes.

15 donkey _____ey ov_____

16 lion _____raw_____

17 goose _____quack_____

18 hen _____wk_____

Write two *antonyms* for each of these words.

19–20 tidy _____untidy_____ _____messy_____

21–22 happy _____unhappy_____ _____upset_____

23–24 strong _____weak_____ _____

25–26 dry _____wet_____ _____damp_____

Choose a word to complete each expression.

fence   cloud   music   cats

27 Every _____fence_____ has a silver lining.

28 It is raining _____cats_____ and dogs.

29 To sit on the _____cloud_____.

30 To face the _____music_____.

Total

TEST 16: **Mixed**

Test time: 0 |||||||||| 5 |||||||||| 10 minutes

Write the *abbreviations* of these words.

1   His Royal Highness   HRH

2   do it yourself   DIY

3   December   DB

4   Prime Minister   PM

5   old age pensioner   OAP

6   Post Office   PO

Add 'to', 'too' or 'two' to each sentence to make it correct.

7   The chips were ___to___ hot.

8   ___too___ many people were trying to get on the bus.

9–10   Danielle wanted ___to___ go ___too___ Rupa's party.

11   The ___two___ boys ran as fast as they could.

12   The teacher spoke sternly ___too___ the giggling children.

Rewrite these sentences with the missing punctuation.

13–16   Time for your piano lesson Mum called

"Time for your piano lesson," Mum called.

17–20   Where have you put my phone asked Rebecca

"Where have you put my phone?" asked Rebecca

Add an interesting *adjective* to describe each of these *nouns*.

21 the _beautiful_ dress

22 the _spicky_ hedgehog

23 the _bright_ professor

24 the _fancy_ restaurant

Use *connectives* to write each of these pairs of short sentences as one sentence.

25 The rain poured. They still had a BBQ.

The rain poured but they still had a BBQ.

26 There was a fire in the school hall. It didn't do much damage.

There was a fire in the school hall thankfully it didn't do much damage.

27 Jake threw the ball. It landed in someone's garden.

Jake threw the ball and it landed in someone's garden.

Write an *antonym* for each of these words.

28 respect _disrespect_

29 clever _stupid_

30 scream _silent_

TEST 17: Grammar

Test time: 0 ⋯ 5 ⋯ 10 minutes

Complete the table using some of the *nouns* in the short passage.

1–8 Jake had a dislike of insects. He worried that swarms or colonies might attack him! Tyrone wanted to help him get over his fear and so told him to think of them as pets!

Common nouns	Proper nouns	Collective nouns	Abstract nouns
Insects	Jake Tyro?	swarms	Dislike
Pets	Tyron	Colonies	Fear

Write an *adjectival phrase* about each of these *nouns*.

9 a book

A broken small book.

10 the summer

The boring cold summer.

11 an acrobat

An old yeti wrickly acrobat

12 India

The boiling hot India

13 a photograph

A worn destroyed photograph.

Complete each sentence by adding a different *conjunction*.

14 Faye couldn't go to the party ___because___ she was unwell.

15 The flowers opened in the sun ___but___ there was a cold wind blowing.

16 Annie was painting in the kitchen ___when___ the cat had taken cover under the table!

17 Gareth was terrified ___whilst___ the spider made its way towards him.

18 They missed their train ___so___ they had to catch a bus.

Circle the *adverbs* and underline the *prepositions* in these sentences.

19–20 Everyone watched (anxiously) as the rope was lowered <u>over</u> the edge of the cliff.

21–22 The children wandered off (gloomily) <u>despite</u> being given some money to spend.

23–24 Nazar worked (happily) knowing as soon as he'd finished cleaning the car he could go <u>inside</u> to watch the rugby match.

Write three sentences, each including two *possessive pronouns*.

25–26 Derek played games despite his dad telling him not to.

27–28 James put on her mum's perfume knowing it was hers.

29–30 Jake ran for his life when his friend stalked him down.

35

Total

Read this article carefully.

The Kamaus from Kenya   *by Xan Rice*

1 For the half-term holidays, the Kamaus
went upcountry to the farming village
where Pauline's parents live. Though
just 60 miles from the Kenyan capital,
5 Nairobi, Murang'a is a very different
world.

Tarred road gives way to dirt; concrete
urban sprawl to rich red soil. The
background noise comes from cockerels
10 and cows rather than the car hooters
and blaring radios of the big city.

The children love visiting their
grandparents. Though Joyce is
something of a TV addict, she and
15 Sharon revel in the wide-open space
and the chance to play all day with their
cousins, who seldom make it to Nairobi.

They also practise speaking Kikuyu,
which should be their mother tongue.
20 Boniface and Pauline are native Kikuyu
speakers, but at home in Nairobi
they communicate in Kiswahili, which
together with English is Kenya's official
national language and predominates in
25 the urban areas. At school, Joyce learns
only the two national languages, and her
Kikuyu is rusty at best....

Pauline also enjoys being home with her
parents. As their first-born child, she
30 assumes the greatest responsibility of all
her siblings for her parents' well-being.
For now they are doing just fine.

On a hectare of land, they grow maize,
beans, bananas, sugarcane, sweet
35 potatoes, avocados and coffee. They
also have a cow, a few goats, chickens
and rabbits. Some of the produce is
eaten; the rest taken to the wholesale
market.

40 Pauline quickly slipped back into the
lifestyle of her youth. She fetched
water from the nearby stream. She
worked in the fields. In the evenings,
she helped prepare dinner. It made her
45 nostalgic, and after the holiday Pauline
told Boniface that they should think of
moving to the countryside.

But Boniface was not tempted. Murang'a
in particular, just a few miles from where
50 he was raised, holds too many memories
of a difficult childhood. Then there is
the issue of work. Being a taxi-driver
in Nairobi is a tough job, but at least it
provides a steady income – far more
55 than he could ever make as a small-
scale farmer.

Article from the Guardian *by Xan Rice*

Answer these questions about the article.

1 Where do the Kamaus live in Kenya?

Nairobi

2 List two differences between life in Murang'a and life in Nairobi.

_____

_____

3 Who is Joyce?

Daughter of Boniface

4 What is a 'mother tongue' (line 19)?

Native language

5 What do you notice about the foods grown in Murang'a compared to in England?

Group of plants

6 Why do you think Pauline wanted to move back to the countryside?

It felt safer.

7–8 Describe two ways the life of these children's grandparents differs from the lives of the grandparents of many children in the United Kingdom.

The grandparents had to get water them selves. The grandp-arents in England use a tap.

_____

9 What is meant by the sentence 'Then there is the issue of work' (lines 51–52)?

Get a job to get the money herely.

10 How many similarities can you list between your family and the Kamaus family?

Love eachother each other, watching TV, Respecting each other.

Total

Write a *synonym* for each of the words in bold.

1   Please pass me the **part** of the newspaper that is for children.

_____

2   The bungalow in our street has been **vacant** for a year. _____

3   She is so **stingy**, she never shares her colouring pens. _____

4   It was **clear** from his pale face that he had hurt his ankle badly.

_____ovious_____

5   Gemma, can you **remember** what I asked you to do next?

_____recall_____

Write the *plural* forms of these words.

6   torch   _torchess_   9   bike   _bikes_

7   princess   _princesses_   10   valley   _vallies_

8   thief   _thiefs_   11   suffix   _suffixes_

Circle the *preposition* in each of these sentences.

12   George's shoes were hidden (under) the sofa.

13   Tea will be ready (at) six-thirty.

14   Helen mended her broken tyre with a puncture repair kit.

15   The river flooded (above) the height of the fence posts.

16   The dog slept soundly (on) his owner's bed!

Change these words into *verbs* by adding a *suffix*.

en   ise   ify

17 drama _dramaify_

18 solid _solidify_

19 thick _thicken_

20 fertile _fertilise_

Add the missing apostrophes.

21 You'll have to learn your spellings for the test!

22 We mustn't be late.

23 Let's buy some sweets, please.

24 You could've stayed longer.

25 I wish I'd brought my bike to ride.

Write a word with the same letter string as underlined in each of these words, but a different pronunciation.

26 t<u>ough</u> _dough_

27 h<u>eight</u> _eight_

28 br<u>own</u> _owns_

29 f<u>our</u> _ours_

30 sp<u>oon</u> _door_

Total

> Write two sentences. Each sentence needs to have two commas.

1–2

All of a sudden, Daniel was ~~attached~~ attached, by a weird creature.

3–4

James and Anthony went to Zoe's house, even though it was a school day.

> Write these questions as statements.

5 Is it time to meet in the park?

It is time to meet in the park.

6 Are we going on holiday to Devon?

We are going on holiday, to Devon

7 Did Liverpool win the Premiership?

Liverpool won the premiership.

8 Is the school closed because of the snow that fell last night?

The school closed because of the snow that fell last night.

9 Are the cows milked twice a day?

Cows are milked twice a day.

Add 'is' or 'are' to each sentence to make it correct.

10   On Saturday, Kellie and Sarah __are__ coming for a sleepover.

11   We __are__ still waiting for the train!

12   Hussan __is__ working hard to improve his skateboarding.

13   Daniel __is__ going to walk the dog when he gets home.

14   __Is__ Sam's answer right?

15   Where __are__ your gloves?

Rewrite this short passage correctly.

16–28

what time does the film start asked brenna

she was worried they wouldn't have time to buy popcorn before it started

we have plenty of time her dad reassured her

"What time does the film start?" asked Brenna. "She worried they wouldn't have time to by popcorn before it started. "We have plenty of time her dad reassured her.

Puzzle ❶

Each of these words has within it a number of smaller words.

How many smaller words can you find in each word, without rearranging the letters or missing letters out?

sausage

sage, usage, age

wardrobe

war, robe, ward

mathematics

math, matics, tics

scarecrow

scare, crow, row

coincidentally

coin, tall, dent

Find your own word that has at least five smaller words within it.

Try it out on someone.

28\10\22

Puzzle ❷

Can you find 26 different *adjectives*, each beginning with a different letter of the alphabet?

a _mazing_

b _eautiful_

c _ool_

d _ifferent_

e _negetic_

f _antastic_

g _ive_

h _ide_

i _diot_

j _ump_

k _ind_

l _ove_

m _dan van_

n _ice_

o _xious_

p _erfect_

q _uick_

r _ude_

s _neak_

t _idy_

u _a nique_

v _xious_

w _eird_

x _eric_

y _owng_

z _any_

Circle the five most imaginative *adjectives* you have written.

Puzzle ❸

Answer these problems, then try again using a dictionary!

List as many words as you can that lie alphabetically between the words 'marmalade' and 'measure'.

My unaided answers

My answers with the help of a dictionary

Write the longest word you can think of.

_____

Write the longest word you can find in a dictionary.

_____

Write a word with as many vowels as possible.

_____

Write a word from the dictionary that uses as many vowels as possible.

_____

Can you find a word in the dictionary that uses all of the vowel letters?

_____

Puzzle 4

Look carefully at these words.

spoon   **sister**   **petal**

If the letters in each word are rearranged they will make a new word.
These words are called anagrams.

spoon	=	**snoop**
sister	=	**resist**
petal	=	**plate**

Your challenge is to find the hidden words by rearranging the letters in
these words, as quickly as possible!

north   _____

parties   _____

vowels   _____

team   _____

eighth   _____

thicken   _____

Now make three anagrams of your own.

_____ = _____

_____ = _____

_____ = _____

Puzzle 5

g	f	r	a	t	u	h	m	c	i
s	e	n	s	i	b	l	e	t	p
d	w	e	m	n	s	q	h	o	p
v	h	q	c	y	n	g	c	r	e
t	e	a	k	d	i	y	a	o	g
i	e	j	p	r	k	r	d	u	i
t	w	g	j	p	o	d	s	g	b
e	l	s	i	a	y	n	e	h	y
u	n	o	f	f	i	c	i	a	l
p	i	t	l	e	g	i	b	l	e

Look in the wordsearch to find *antonyms* for the following words.
Write the words you have found.

silly   _____

official   _____

dissatisfied   _____

huge   _____

incorrect   _____

unclear   _____

smooth   _____

Key words

abbreviation	a word that has been shortened
abstract noun	a noun referring to a concept or idea, for example love, beauty
adjectival phrase	a group of words describing a noun
adjective	a word that describes somebody or something
adverb	a word that gives extra meaning to a verb
alphabetical order	words arranged in the order of the letters in the alphabet
antonym	a word with a meaning opposite to another word, for example hot/cold
clause	a section of a sentence with a verb
collective noun	a word referring to a group or collection of things, for example a swarm of bees
common noun	a general name of a person, place or thing, for example boy, office
compound word	a word made up of two other words, for example football
conjunction	a word used to link sentences, phrases or words, for example and, but
connective	a word or words that join clauses or sentences
contraction	two words shortened into one with an apostrophe placed where the letter/s have been dropped, for example do not/don't
definition	the meaning of a word
double negative	two negative words in a sentence that make the idea in the sentence positive, for example I am <u>not</u> going to buy <u>no</u> bike (which means I am going to buy a bike)
homophone	a word that has the same sound as another but a different meaning or spelling, for example right/write
modal verb	a verb that changes the meaning of other verbs, for example can, will
noun	a naming word
onomatopoeic	a word that echoes a sound, associated with its meaning, for example hiss
parenthesis	this is a word or phrase that is separated off from the main sentence by brackets, commas or dashes usually because it contains additional information not essential to its understanding
phrase	a group of words that do not contain both a subject and a verb
plural	more than one, for example cats
possessive pronoun	a pronoun showing to whom something belongs, for example mine, ours
prefix	a group of letters added to the beginning of a word, for example un, dis
preposition	a word that links nouns and pronouns to other parts of a sentence, for example he sat *behind* the door
pronoun	a word that can be used instead of a noun
proper noun	the specific name or title of a person or a place, for example Ben, London
relative clause	a special type of clause that makes the meaning of a noun more specific, for example The prize *that I won* was a book
reported speech	what has been said without using the exact words or speech marks
root word	a word to which a prefix or suffix can be added to make another word, for example quick – *quickly*
singular	one of something, for example cat
suffix	a group of letters added to the end of a word, for example ly, ful
synonym	a word with a very similar meaning to another word, for example quick/fast
tense	tells when an action was done, for example past (*I slept*), present (*I am sleeping*) or future (*I will sleep*)
verb	a 'doing' or 'being' word

Total

Progress Grid

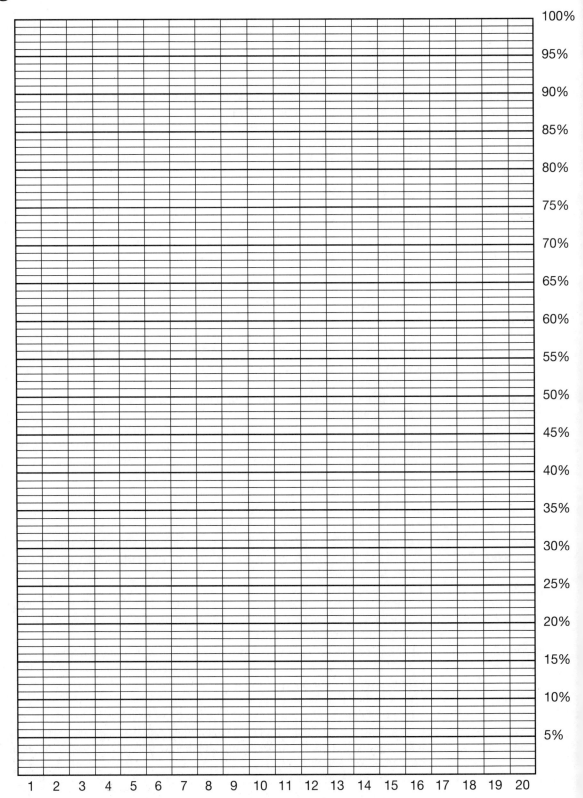

Total marks

Test